Mastering the Art of Sandwich Making

Tiarna .G Mccartney

All rights reserved.

Copyright © 2024 Tiarna .G Mccartney

Mastering the Art of Sandwich Making : Crafting Delicious and Unique Sandwiches - Expert Techniques and Recipes for your Kitchen

Funny helpful tips:

Practice critical reading; question the author's intent and evaluate the content's validity.

Stay committed to growth; evolving together strengthens the bond.

<u>Life advices:</u>

Practice patience; good things often take time.

Your journey is a reflection of your spirit's resilience; embrace each step with gratitude and pride.

Introduction

This is a culinary guide that unlocks the creative potential of the breakfast sandwich maker, a kitchen appliance designed to simplify and enhance the morning meal preparation. This cookbook offers a diverse range of breakfast sandwich recipes that cater to various tastes and dietary preferences.

The book begins by highlighting the benefits of using a breakfast sandwich maker, emphasizing its convenience and versatility in crafting delicious morning meals. It then dives into the heart of the cookbook, presenting a wide array of breakfast sandwich recipes, each categorized into different sections to suit individual preferences.

Egg-based breakfast sandwich recipes take center stage, offering a variety of options like the Egg White and Mozzarella English Muffin, Fried Egg and Cheese Bagel, and Eggs Parmesan English Muffin. These recipes showcase the versatility of eggs as a breakfast staple and provide choices for both classic and inventive flavors.

For those who prefer fruit-inspired breakfasts, the Fruit Breakfast Sandwich Recipes section offers delightful options such as the Blueberry and Pear Croissant and the Apple, Cheddar, and Cinnamon-Raisin Sandwich. These recipes introduce the sweetness of fruits to breakfast sandwiches, adding a refreshing twist to the morning routine.

Vegetarian breakfast sandwich recipes cater to individuals who opt for meatless options, featuring creations like the Vegetarian Omelet Sandwich and the Mediterranean English Muffin Sandwich. These recipes highlight the use of plant-based ingredients, herbs, and spices to deliver satisfying and flavorful breakfast experiences.

The cookbook also includes a selection of meaty breakfast sandwich recipes, satisfying carnivorous cravings with options like the Canadian Bacon and Cheese Croissant, Chorizo and Egg English Muffin, and Polished Sausage, Egg, and Monterey Jack Bagel. These recipes showcase various meat-based protein sources that can be incorporated into breakfast sandwiches.

For those seeking a breakfast with a twist, the Waffle and Pancake Breakfast Sandwich Recipes section offers inventive combinations such as the Pineapple, Bacon Waffle Sandwich and the Chicken and Bacon Waffle Sandwich. These recipes demonstrate how waffles and pancakes can serve as delightful bread alternatives in breakfast sandwiches.

The cookbook further explores tortilla-based breakfast sandwiches with options like the Mushroom, Egg, and Bacon Flour Tortilla and the Avocado, Black Bean, and Egg Corn Tortilla. These recipes embrace the flavors of different cuisines and introduce a touch of international flair to the breakfast table.

In closing, this book is a comprehensive guide that caters to a wide range of breakfast preferences, from classic to innovative. It empowers readers to make the most of their breakfast sandwich maker by offering a diverse collection of recipes that can brighten up their morning routines. Whether you're an egg enthusiast, a fruit lover, a vegetarian, or a meat aficionado, this cookbook provides a delightful selection of breakfast sandwich ideas that will surely kickstart your day with flavor and satisfaction.

Contents

Benefits of Using a BreakfastSandwich Maker 1

Eggs Breakfast Sandwich Recipes 4

Egg White and Mozzarella EnglishMuffin 5

Fried Egg and Cheese Bagel 7

Buttermilk Biscuit with Eggs 9

Eggs Parmesan English Muffin 11

Egg Salad and Pepperjack EnglishMuffin 13

Fruit Breakfast Sandwich Recipes 16

Blueberry and Pear Croissant (pear-berry) 17

Apple, Cheddar and Cinnamon-RaisinSandwich 19

Ricotta and Peach Breakfast Biscuit(Peach ricotta basil) 22

Apple, Bacon, Egg and CheeseCroissant 25

Chocolate Raspberry SourdoughSandwich 28

Apricot and Brie Croissant 30

Peanut Butter & Banana EnglishMuffin 32

Vegetarian Breakfast SandwichRecipes 34

Vegetarian Omelet Sandwich 35

Mediterranean English MuffinSandwich 38

Egg Florentine English Muffin 41

Taste of Italy Bagel Sandwich 43

Eggs, Beans and Cheese on Wheat 45

Dates, Goat Cheese Vegetarian Bagel 47

Scrambled Egg and Avocado EnglishMuffin 49

Vegetarian Patty Sandwich 52

Red Pepper and Spinach on Wheat..55
Meat Breakfast Sandwich Recipes 57
Lox and Egg Breakfast Bagel..59
Canadian Bacon and CheeseCroissant 62
Parmesan and Bacon Whole WheatSandwich 64
Basic Bacon, Egg and Cheese Bagel 67
Chopped Ham and Basil OmeletSandwich 69
Chorizo and Egg English Muffin..72
Healthy Turkey Bacon, Egg WhiteEnglish Muffin 75
Bacon and Fried Potato EnglishMuffin...77
Loaded Omelet Croissant 80
Eggs Benedict Bagel...83
Chipotle Bacon, Egg and CheeseBiscuit 86
Polish Sausage, Egg and MontereyJack Bagel 90
Waffle and Pancake BreakfastSandwich Recipes 92
Pineapple, Bacon Waffle Sandwich...93
Sausage, Egg and Cheese WaffleSandwich 95
Ham, Egg, Cheese and ButtermilkPancake Sandwich 97
Cream Cheese and Raspberry WaffleSandwich 99
Sausage, Pancake and SyrupSandwich 102
Chicken and Bacon Waffle Sandwich..104
Tortilla Based Breakfast Sandwiches 107
Mushroom, Egg and Bacon FlourTortilla...108
Mexican Corn Tortilla Sandwich 111
Spinach, Tomato and Egg FlourTortilla 114
Fried Potatoes and Egg Tortilla 116
Black Bean and Corn Salsa FlourTortilla 118

Avocado, Black Bean and Egg CornTortilla..120
Enjoy Your New Breakfast Regime 123

Benefits of Using a Breakfast Sandwich Maker

Before delving into the breakfast sandwich maker recipes, it is important to understand why using a breakfast sandwich maker for these recipes is such a great idea. Sure, you can make breakfast sandwiches without a sandwich maker, but purchasing, and using, a breakfast sandwich maker offers many great benefits that make it easier for you to ensure you and your family are enjoying a health breakfast every day. Here is a look at just a few of the benefits you can enjoy when you use a breakfast sandwich maker in your own home.

Benefit #1 – Lets You Create Healthier Breakfasts

A breakfast sandwich maker allows you to create healthier breakfasts, which is one of the great benefits to having this kitchen appliance. With the sandwich maker, you do not have to use butter or oil when making the sandwich, ensuring you have a healthier sandwich. However, some recipes may call for a little butter or cooking spray. Since sandwich makers are made with non-stick materials, butter or oil is not required when making your sandwich. Reducing your fat intake can lower cholesterol and help prevent future heart problems.

With the breakfast sandwich maker, you can easily create a breakfast with ingredients you put together on your own. This keeps you from having to choose unhealthy breakfast options, such as sugary cereals or fast food sandwiches.

Benefit #2 – It's Easy to Use

Another benefit of the breakfast sandwich maker is that it is so easy to use. When it comes to cooking breakfast for you or your entire family, you want to make sure it is as easy as possible. After all, mornings can be hectic. You do not have time to deal with a complicated breakfast. Breakfast sandwich makers are so easy that you will only need to preheat the appliance, add the ingredients and then wait for your sandwich to cook. They also come with helpful instructions from the manufacturer that you can review to make the process even easier.

Benefit #3 – You Will Save Time

Having a breakfast sandwich maker in your home will save you a huge amount of time in the morning, which is one of the most popular benefits it has to offer. Even if you do not think you have time for breakfast, this appliance allows you to quickly make breakfast in just a few minutes. Simply preheat it for a few minutes while you are getting ready for the day, then add the ingredients and give it a few more minutes to cook. You will have a great sandwich in no time.

Benefit #4 – Easy to Clean

Many breakfast sandwich maker users note that they love how easy to clean these appliances are. They easily come apart so you can clean each part of the appliance. Wash the parts by hand or throw them in the dishwasher if you are short on time. There is no big mess to clean up when using this appliance to create your breakfast each day.

Benefit #5 – Durable and Compact

The durability and compact design are both important benefits of the breakfast sandwich maker. These appliances use a special non-stick coating to ensure that foods do not stick to the appliance, helping to make the device last even longer. Most breakfast sandwich makers come with a warranty as well. Surprisingly, these appliances are also compact, so you can easily store it. It fits nicely in kitchen cupboards or you can store it on the countertop with easy, since it only takes a small amount of space.

Benefit #6 – Easy to Experiment

Lastly, a breakfast sandwich maker makes it easy to experiment with new recipes. The design of the appliance makes it easy for you to try using different sandwich breads, various fillings and more. Have fun trying new recipes and using new ingredients. It will keep breakfast fun and ensure you do not get bored eating the same old breakfast every day.

Eggs Breakfast Sandwich Recipes

Eggs offer a great way to get protein for breakfast. There is something delicious and comforting about a warm egg sandwich, whether you have the eggs alone on a bagel or English muffin, or you decide to add some cheese or other toppings. The great thing about your breakfast sandwich maker is that it easily cooks your eggs in no time, making them in a perfect circle so the eggs fit the sandwich and will not slide off. If you want a simple, egg sandwich, try one of these tasty recipes.

Egg White and Mozzarella English Muffin

If you are looking for a low calorie, low fat breakfast sandwich, then this sandwich is a great choice. It only uses egg whites, so it really cuts the fat and calories while still offering plenty of protein. Low fat mozzarella cheese is used as well to add flavor without adding a lot of fat to the sandwich. While this recipe only makes one sandwich, you can always double or triple the recipe if you are making breakfast for the whole family.

Ingredients:

- 1 whole wheat English muffin, cut in half
- 2 large eggs, egg whites only
- 1 slice of low fat mozzarella cheese

How to Make It:

Start by preheating your breakfast sandwich maker. The ready light should come on when it is done preheating.

Add the bottom half of your English muffin to the bottom ring of the appliance, making sure the cut side is facing up.

Place the slice of low fat mozzarella cheese on the English muffin.

Next, in the egg cooking plate, add the egg whites.

In the top ring, place the top of the English muffin, placing the cut side down.

Close the sandwich maker and allow to cook for about five minutes.

Carefully pull out the egg cooking plate, then open the sandwich maker and remove the sandwich carefully.

Servings:

Makes 1 serving

Fried Egg and Cheese Bagel

Do you love the taste of fried eggs? If so, you will love this delicious sandwich. You only have to use a small amount of butter to get the fried egg flavor, which makes this recipe lower in fat than a traditional fried egg sandwich. While the recipe calls for American cheese, you can always use a slice of your favorite cheese instead. Use a plain bagel with the recipe, or try a cheese, onion or loaded bagel for a slightly different flavor.

Ingredients:

- 1 plain bagel, sliced
- 1 egg
- 1 pat of butter
- 1 slice of American cheese
- Ketchup to taste (optional)

How to Make It:

Preheat your sandwich maker until it is ready.

Take the bottom of the sliced bagel, placing it in the bottom ring of the sandwich maker.

Place the slice of American cheese on top of the bagel bottom.

In the egg slot, place a tiny pat of butter and then crack an egg onto the cooking plate.

In the top slot, add the top of the bagel.

Close the appliance and cook until eggs reach your desired consistency. If you like the yolks hard, cook for about five minutes. If you want your fried egg over easy, then reduce cooking time by a minute or so.

Slip out the cooking plate, then carefully open and remove the sandwich.

Eat immediately.

Servings:

Makes 1 serving

Buttermilk Biscuit with Eggs

Breakfast biscuits are so delicious and they are the perfect base for a simple egg sandwich. Just make sure you choose biscuits that are large enough for the breakfast sandwich maker. Use canned buttermilk biscuits to quickly make the biscuits that you need, or you can make your own homemade buttermilk biscuits to use with this recipe. If you are going to be in a hurry in the morning, make the biscuits ahead of time to make the preparation time even faster.

Ingredients:

- 1 buttermilk biscuit, cut in half
- 1 slice of sharp cheddar cheese
- 1 egg
- Milk
- Salt and pepper to taste

How to Make It:

In a bowl, crack the egg and add a bit of milk. Add a dash of salt and pepper for flavor. Use a whisk to whisk the egg and milk together.

Make sure the breakfast sandwich maker is preheated.

Take the bottom of the biscuit, placing it in the bottom slot of the breakfast sandwich maker.

Top the bottom of the biscuit with the slice of cheddar cheese.

Pour the egg mixture into the egg slot.

Place the biscuit top in the top slot of the sandwich maker.

Close and cook for about five minutes.

Remove cooking plate, open the appliance and carefully take out the sandwich.

Remove the top of the biscuit and add ketchup if desired.

Enjoy while warm.

Servings:

Makes 1 serving

Eggs Parmesan English Muffin

Enjoy the rich taste of parmesan cheese and a bit of marinara sauce with this tasty egg sandwich. You only need a little parmesan to get great flavor and the marinara sauce gives a nice dose of vitamins and minerals too. Make your own tomato sauce or buy canned marinara sauce for the recipe. You will enjoy getting a nice Italian flavor for breakfast.

Ingredients:

- 1 English muffin (whole grain is best), split
- 1 large egg
- 1/8 cup of parmesan cheese
- 1/4 cup of marinara sauce

How to Make It:

Begin by preheating the breakfast sandwich maker until the ready light comes on.

When the appliance is ready, open and add the bottom of the English muffin to the bottom slot.

Top the bottom of the English muffin with the cup of marinara sauce.

Sprinkle the cup of parmesan cheese on top of the sauce.

Next, add the egg to the cooking plate.

Add the top of the English muffin to the top slot.

Close and cook for 4-5 minutes, giving the egg time to cook and the sauce and cheese time to warm.

Remove the cooking plate and then open the appliance, taking the sandwich out carefully.

Enjoy the sandwich while hot.

Servings:

Makes 1 serving

Egg Salad and Pepperjack English Muffin

Warm egg salad gets a kick from the pepperjack cheese. The recipe is easy and fast, making it easy for you to get your morning started with a nutritious breakfast. Using Greek yogurt instead of mayo helps reduce calories and fat. Add green onions or even a little hot pepper sauce for an extra kick when making this sandwich recipe.

Ingredients:

- 2 whole grain English muffins, split
- ¼ cup of Greek yogurt
- 1 teaspoon of horseradish
- 2 teaspoons of honey
- 2 teaspoons of Dijon mustard
- Ground pepper to taste
- Salt to taste
- 3 hard boiled eggs, chopped roughly
- 1/3 cup of pepperjack cheese, shredded (or use 2 slices)

How to Make It:

Preheat the sandwich maker.

In a bowl, combine together the Greek yogurt, horseradish, honey, Dijon mustard, pepper, salt and hard boiled eggs. Stir together until well combined.

Remove the cooking plate; you will not need it.

Take the English muffin bottom, placing it cut side up in the bottom slot of the sandwich maker.

Place about ½ the cheese on top of the English muffin bottom.

Then, spoon half of the egg salad mixture on top of the cheese.

Place the top of the English muffin in the top slot.

Cook for 3-5 minutes, or until egg salad is warm and cheese has melted.

Repeat with the rest of the ingredients.

Eat while warm.

Servings:

Makes 2 servings

Fruit Breakfast Sandwich Recipes

Many people never think of making breakfast sandwiches that include fruit. Fruits offer many important vitamins and minerals to your diet, and many fruits also contain a lot of fiber, which is an important part of a healthy diet. If you are craving a sweet breakfast, these breakfast sandwich recipes are sure to help curb your sweet tooth in a healthy way. Enjoy these tasty combinations of fruits and other ingredients. These sandwiches are so good that you will not just want to eat them at breakfast time. They make wonderful snacks too.

Blueberry and Pear Croissant (pear-berry)

When you are craving a sweet dish for breakfast, this sandwich offers a delicious, sweet pairing of pears and blueberries. The pears offer plenty of fiber and blueberries are packed with antioxidants. When added to a flaky, warm croissant, you have a perfect sandwich that is ready in minutes. Although the recipe calls for adding the fruit to the sandwich and warming it with the rest of the sandwich, you can always add the fruit last if you think you would enjoy it better cold.

Ingredients:

- 2 medium croissants, sliced in half
- 1 large pear (bosc pears are a perfect choice), thinly sliced
- 2 tablespoons of honey
- ½ cup of blueberries, rinsed, drained and dried
- 3 tablespoons of cream cheese, brought to room temperature

How to Make It:

Preheat the sandwich maker.

Take 1 ½ teaspoons of the cream cheese, spreading half of it on the top of the croissant and half on the croissant bottom.

Place the croissant bottom in the bottom slot of the sandwich maker, topped with half of the pear slices.

Add ¼ cup of blueberries on top of the pear slices.

Take a tablespoon of the honey, drizzling it carefully over the fruit.

Then, place the croissant top in the top slot of the appliance.

Close and cook for 3 minutes, ensuring the fruit has softened and the cream cheese has melted.

Repeat with the rest of the ingredients.

Remove carefully and eat while warm.

Servings:

Makes 2 servings

Apple, Cheddar and Cinnamon-Raisin Sandwich

Apples and cheddar cheese always make a great combination. This recipe combines those two ingredients with the delicious flavor of cinnamon-raisin bread as well, creating a delightful sandwich that is full of flavor. The fiber of the bread and apple will keep you full, while the cheddar cheese provides some protein. While this recipe only makes a single serving, it is so good that you will definitely want to double or triple the recipe to feed this delightful sandwich to the entire family. It makes a great option for a nice brunch as well.

Ingredients:

- 1 cinnamon raisin bagel
- ½ medium granny smith apple, thinly sliced
- 1 slice of sharp cheddar cheese

How to Make It:

Start by preheating the breakfast sandwich maker.

While the appliance is preheating, slice half of an apple very thinly.

Slice the bagel as well.

Take the bottom of the bagel and place it in the bottom of the sandwich maker.

Remove the cooking plate, since you will not need it for this recipe.

Top the bottom of the bagel with the thin slices of apple.

Place the slice of sharp cheddar on top of the apple slices.

Add the top of the bagel to the top slot.

Cook for 3-4 minutes, ensuring that the cheese is nicely melted.

Open and carefully take the sandwich out.

Enjoy immediately.

Servings:

Makes 1 serving

Ricotta and Peach Breakfast Biscuit (Peach ricotta basil)

Ricotta cheese always pairs well with fruits and tastes wonderful with the peaches used within this breakfast sandwich recipe. Peaches are wonderful for you, since they have a nice dose of vitamin C and potassium. Potassium helps to keep blood pressure normal and the vitamin C gives your immune system a boost as well. Sweetened with just a bit of honey, this recipe is sweet but still good for you.

Ingredients:

- 1 breakfast biscuit, homemade or canned, sliced
- 1 yellow peach, peeled and thinly sliced
- 1 tablespoon of ricotta cheese
- 1 tablespoon of honey
- 1 tablespoon of sugar, optional and to taste

How to Make It:

Wash the peach, then remove the pit and peel the peach.

Slice the peach in very thin slices.

Place the peach slices into a medium bowl.

If desired, sprinkle with the sugar, although you can skip this step if you want to.

Allow the peaches to sit in the bowl for about 30 minutes.

Stir the sliced peaches to distribute the peach juice that has accumulated in the bowl.

Take the bottom half of the biscuit and top with a tablespoon of the ricotta cheese.

Add the biscuit bottom to the bottom slot of the sandwich maker.

Drizzle one tablespoon of the honey over the ricotta.

Top with the ricotta and the peaches.

Add the top of the biscuit to the top slot.

Heat for 4-5 minutes, ensuring the sandwich is warm all the way through.

Take out the cooking plate and then take out the sandwich.

Eat while warm.

Servings:

Makes 1 serving

Apple, Bacon, Egg and Cheese Croissant

The combination of apple, bacon, eggs and shredded cheese is a unique one. This croissant gives you bread, dairy, meat, eggs and fruit, all in a single sandwich. The flavors blend for a tasty sandwich that makes any morning feel special. While the recipe calls for a croissant, you can always use an English muffin or a bagel if you do not have a croissant on hand. However, the croissant adds a buttery, flakiness that is wonderful.

Ingredients:

- 2 small croissants
- 2 large eggs
- 1 small Granny Smith apple
- 2 slices of precooked bacon
- ¼ cup of shredded cheddar cheese

How to Make It:

Make sure you preheat the sandwich maker.

Wash apple and then core it.

Slice apple into rounds, making sure slices are very thin. Leave the peel on, since it contains great nutrients.

Slice the croissant, placing the bottom of the croissant into the appliance in the appropriate place.

Top the croissant with ½ of the shredded cheddar cheese.

Place ½ of the apple slices on top of the cheese, then top with 1 slice of the precooked bacon, broken in half to make it fit on the croissant.

Use a whisk to whisk the two eggs together in a bowl.

Place half of the egg mixture on the cooking plate.

Take the top of the croissant, adding it to the top slot.

Close the appliance and allow to cook for five minutes, ensuring eggs are fully cooked.

When done, remove the cooking plate, then take the sandwich out and enjoy eating it while warm.

Repeat the process with the second croissant.

Servings:

Makes 2 servings

Chocolate Raspberry Sourdough Sandwich

If you enjoy the combination of fruit and chocolate, you will appreciate this incredible sandwich. Add the combination of creamy brie and you really have a gourmet breakfast hit. Not only will you want to enjoy this sandwich yourself, but it is a delightful option for guests if you are hosting a brunch. Raspberries offer plenty of antioxidants and vitamins, and the hazelnut, chocolate spread adds a dessert like flavor to the sandwich.

Ingredients:

- 2 slices of sourdough bread
- 1 tablespoon of Nutella, or other chocolate, hazelnut spread
- ½ cup of fresh raspberries, washed, drained and dried
- 2 tablespoons of soft brie cheese

How to Make It:

Take the time to make sure the breakfast sandwich maker is preheated.

Take the sourdough bread slices and use a cookie cutter or large glass to cut the bread into circles that will fit into the sandwich maker.

Spread the Nutella on one slice of the bread.

Place the brie on top of the Nutella, then add all this to the bottom slot of the sandwich maker.

Add the raspberries on top of the brie and then add the top slice of the sourdough bread in the top slot.

Cook for five minutes, ensuring bread is nicely toasted and the brie has melted.

Remove from the sandwich maker.

Be sure to eat the sandwich while it is warm.

Servings:

Makes 1 serving

Apricot and Brie Croissant

This combination of brie and apricot preserves makes a delicious treat for breakfast that will seem like dessert. Serve it up when you want a warm, sweet breakfast or make it for a brunch when you have guests in your home. While the sandwich tastes like you spent a lot of time working on it, it really is easy to make and you can have these sandwiches complete in no time. You may want to double or triple the recipe, depending on how many people you need to serve.

Ingredients:

- 1 medium croissant
- ½ teaspoon of dark brown sugar
- Cinnamon to taste
- 1 ounce of brie, cut into slices, rind removed
- ½ tablespoon of chopped, glazed pecans
- 1 tablespoon of apricot preserves

How to Make It:

Preheat the sandwich maker, so it can be warming while you prepare the rest of the sandwich.

Slice the croissant.

Take the bottom of the croissant and cover it with the brie.

Spread the apricot preserves on top of the cheese.

Place the croissant bottom in the bottom slot of the sandwich maker, topping with the pecans and the dark brown sugar.

Sprinkle with a bit of cinnamon.

Put the top of the croissant into the top slot of the appliance.

Allow to cook for about 5 minutes, ensuring that the croissant is nicely browned.

Remove sandwich and eat while still warm.

Servings:

Makes 1 serving

Peanut Butter & Banana English Muffin

Bananas and peanut butter go together wonderfully. In fact, banana and peanut butter grilled sandwiches are popular, especially with kids. If you want to serve up a healthy breakfast that the kids will love, then this peanut butter and banana English muffin are sure to please. The great thing is that it is actually a healthy choice. You will enjoy whole grains from the English muffin, a great dose of potassium and vitamins from the banana and healthy fats and protein from the peanut butter.

Ingredients:

- 1 Whole grain English muffin, sliced
- 2 tablespoons of peanut butter
- 1 small banana, thinly sliced

How to Make It:

Start by making sure the breakfast sandwich maker is preheated.

Slice the English muffin, spreading the peanut butter on the bottom.

Add the English muffin bottom to the sandwich maker.

Top it with the sliced bananas.

Add the top of the English muffin in the top slot, then cook for four minutes, ensuring the sandwich is heated all the way through.

Remove the peanut butter and banana sandwich.

Enjoy warm.

Servings:

Makes 1 serving

Vegetarian Breakfast Sandwich Recipes

If you are a vegetarian or you simply like to avoid eating meat a couple days of the week, these vegetarian breakfast sandwich recipes are the perfect option. These recipes offer the addition of delicious veggies to your sandwich, avoiding meat and providing you with a healthy, delicious breakfast. Even the kids will enjoy these sandwiches, since they are full of wonderful flavors and healthy ingredients.

Vegetarian Omelet Sandwich

Omelets are delicious and it is easy to make a vegetarian omelet that is packed with plenty of veggie goodness. This recipe takes a vegetarian omelet and turns it into a delicious breakfast sandwich that can be enjoyed on the go. With mushrooms, bell peppers, onions and spinach in the omelet, you will get a nice dose of important vitamins and other nutrients from the veggies. The eggs give you plenty of protein and the Havarti cheese gives the sandwich a tasty flavor that you will appreciate. Within minutes, you will have a tasty, healthy breakfast that fits well into your vegetarian lifestyle.

Ingredients:

- 4 whole wheat bagels
- 1 cup of red bell pepper, chopped
- 4 green onions, thinly sliced
- 1 cup of chopped red onion
- 1 cup of chopped baby bella mushrooms
- 8 eggs, well beaten
- 1 cup of Havarti cheese, shredded
- 4 tablespoons of sour cream
- Ground pepper and salt to taste

How to Make It:

Begin by making sure that you preheat the sandwich maker before you get started.

In a skillet, sauté the bell pepper, green onions, red onion and mushrooms in a bit of olive oil or with a bit of cooking spray. Cook until the veggies are tender. Set aside.

In a small bowl, combine the eight eggs, Havarti cheese, salt, pepper and sour cream. Beat until the mixture is combined.

Place the bottom of one whole wheat bagel in the bottom slot of the sandwich maker.

In the egg slot, place ¼ of the egg mixture. Top with the top of the whole wheat bagel.

Cook in the breakfast sandwich maker for about five minutes, ensuring that the eggs cook all the way through.

Take out the egg plate and then carefully remove the sandwich from the appliance.

Repeat the process with the remaining 3 bagels. Enjoy while hot.

Servings:

Makes 4 servings

Mediterranean English Muffin Sandwich

Studies show that individuals eating a Mediterranean diet are healthier and in many cases, slimmer. Why not add some delicious Mediterranean ingredients to your breakfast sandwich for a healthy sandwich that will keep you feeling full while giving you plenty of energy for your day. You get extra vitamins and antioxidants with the olives, cucumber, onions and spinach. A bot of crumbled feta cheese adds flavor.

Ingredients:

- 2 English Muffins (whole grain muffins are the healthiest)
- 10 slices of cucumber
- 1 small tomato, diced
- 2 tablespoons of feta cheese, crumbled
- 4 tablespoons of skim milk
- 2 whole eggs and 4 egg whites
- ¼ cup of kalamata olives, finely chopped
- ½ cup of red onion, finely chopped
- ½ cup of baby spinach leaves, washed, drained and dried

How to Make It:

Before you begin working on the recipe, preheat the sandwich maker.

In a medium bowl, whisk together the milk and all the eggs until combined.

Add the cucumber, onion, tomato, olives and baby spinach leaves to the egg mixture, mixing until the mixture is combined and the veggies are well spread throughout the mixture.

Slice the English muffins.

Take one English muffin bottom and place it in the bottom slot. Top with a tablespoon of the feta cheese.

Pour half of the egg mixture on the egg plate.

In the top slot, add the English muffin top.

Cook for five minutes, ensuring the eggs are well cooked. Remove the egg plate and then take out the sandwich with care.

Repeat the process with the second English muffin.

Eat while the sandwiches are hot.

Servings:

Makes 2 servings

Egg Florentine English Muffin

Did you know that you can create your own delicious egg Florentine sandwich in your sandwich maker? You will enjoy this delicious vegetarian recipe, especially with the combination of baby spinach, mozzarella cheese and delicious eggs. The baby spinach adds great nutrients to the sandwich and if you use low fat mozzarella cheese, you will reduce the calories and fat of the sandwich. Use a whole grain English muffin and you will get plenty of fiber too.

Ingredients:

- 1 English muffin, preferable whole grain
- 1 large egg
- ¼ cup of baby spinach leaves
- 1 slice of low fat Mozzarella cheese
- Ground black pepper and salt to taste

How to Make It:

Preheat the breakfast sandwich maker.

Slice the English muffin in half.

Take the English muffin bottom and top it with the slice of cheese. Place it into the bottom slot.

Place the egg into the egg slot. Sprinkle the egg with a bit of salt and pepper if desired.

Top with the English muffin top.

Cook until the egg yolk reaches your desired doneness.

Remove the egg plate. Then take the sandwich out of the breakfast sandwich maker.

Take the top of the English muffin off, adding the baby spinach leaves on top.

Enjoy right away.

Servings:

Makes 1 serving

Taste of Italy Bagel Sandwich

When you make this delicious breakfast sandwich, you will get a real taste of Italy, using some of the most common Italian combinations of flavors. This sandwich combines tomatoes, mozzarella, olive oil and basil leaves into one delicious sandwich. If you are a vegetarian, this is a great vegetarian breakfast sandwich that is packed with flavor and nutritious goodness. The whole family is going to appreciate this delicious twist on an Italian favorite.

Ingredients:

- 2 whole wheat bagels
- 4 slices of tomato
- 4 slices of low fat mozzarella cheese
- 1 cup of fresh basil leaves, stems removed and washed
- 2 cloves of garlic, finely chopped
- 2 tablespoons of olive oil
- 2 tablespoons of balsamic vinegar

How to Make It:

Be sure to preheat the sandwich maker.

Take the bottom half of one whole wheat bagel, placing it in the bottom slot of the sandwich maker.

Top with two slices of tomato, and then add two slices of the low fat mozzarella cheese.

Add the bagel top in the top slot. Allow to cook for 4-5 minutes, ensuring that the cheese melts.

In a medium bowl, whisk together the finely chopped garlic, the olive oil and the balsamic vinegar.

Once the sandwich is done, remove it from the sandwich maker.

Remove the top of the bagel, topping sandwich with ½ cup of the fresh basil leaves.

Repeat with the remaining ingredients.

Serve sandwiches while warm with the olive oil and balsamic vinaigrette, dipping the bagel in the mixture for a delicious flavor.

Servings:

Makes 2 servings

Eggs, Beans and Cheese on Wheat

The eggs and beans used in this delicious sandwich give you plenty of protein without using any meat, which is why it makes a great vegetarian breakfast sandwich. The combination of flavors are unique and complex, and it is a quick, enjoyable sandwich to try if you are craving something different for breakfast. This recipe only makes a single sandwich, so if you are cooking for a family, you will need to double, triple or quadruple the recipe to fit your family's needs.

Ingredients:

- 2 slices of wheat bread
- 1 slice of medium cheddar cheese
- 2 tablespoons of refried black beans
- 1 large egg

How to Make It:

While working with the ingredients, preheat the sandwich maker.

Use a cookie cutter or a large glass to cut the wheat bread into circles that will work with your breakfast sandwich maker.

Take one piece of bread, placing it into the bottom of your sandwich maker.

Spread the refried black beans over the bread. Top the beans with the slice of medium cheddar cheese.

Add the egg to the egg plate.

Place the other piece of bread in the top slot.

Close the breakfast sandwich maker and cook for 5 minutes, or until the egg is fully cooked.

Carefully take the egg plate out, then remove your sandwich.

Eat immediately to enjoy it while hot.

Servings:

Makes 1 serving

Dates, Goat Cheese Vegetarian Bagel

If you enjoy dates, you are definitely going to love this vegetarian bagel recipe. This sandwich combines some delicious flavors for a very unique sandwich. If you like trying new flavors, you are sure to enjoy giving this recipe a try. The arugula in the recipe gives a peppery flavor to the sandwich, while the dates add a touch of sweetness. The goat cheese also has a unique flavor and it is also low in fat.

Ingredients:

- 2 multigrain bagels, sliced
- ½ cup of rinsed arugula leaves, carefully dried
- 3 tablespoons of goat cheese
- ½ cup of chopped walnuts
- 8 dates, pitted and thinly sliced

How to Make It:

Preheat the sandwich maker.

Take the bottom of one bagel, spreading it with half of the goat cheese. Place into the bottom slot of the appliance.

Sprinkle with half of the walnuts, topping the walnuts with half of the thinly sliced dates.

In the top slot, place the other half of the multigrain bagel.

Cook the sandwich for three minutes. Remove carefully.

Take off the top of the sandwich, adding half of the arugula leaves and then putting the top back on.

Repeat the process with the second multigrain bagel.

Eat warm.

Serving Size:

Makes 2 servings

Scrambled Egg and Avocado English Muffin

Avocados are so good for you, providing healthy fats that are difficult to get in your diet otherwise. The creaminess of the avocadoes makes the sandwich taste decadent without using mayo or other high saturated fat options. This is a great choice for vegetarians or individuals who like to take a break from meat from time to time. Enjoy on a whole wheat English muffin for a healthy, quick breakfast that you can make in just minutes.

Ingredients:

- 4 whole wheat English muffins
- 4 large eggs
- 4 large egg whites
- 1 avocado, pit removed and sliced thinly
- 2 large scallions, finely chopped
- Ground pepper and coarse salt to taste
- Hot sauce to taste (optional)

How to Make It:

Get your breakfast sandwich maker preheating.

In a medium bowl, beat the egg whites and eggs together, adding ground pepper and coarse salt to taste.

Add scallions to the eggs, combining until the scallions are well distributed throughout.

Take 1 English muffin, slicing it. Place the bottom of the English muffin in the bottom slot.

Add ¼ of the egg mixture to the egg plate. Then, add the top of the English muffin in the provided slot.

Cover and cook for five minutes or until eggs are cooked through.

Remove the egg plate, then remove the sandwich with care.

Take the top of the English muffin off the sandwich, topping with ¼ of the slices of avocado.

Place the top back on and serve.

Repeat with the remaining English muffins. Enjoy while warm.

Serving Size:

Makes 4 servings

Vegetarian Patty Sandwich

If you want the protein of meat without eating meat, then the vegetarian breakfast sausage patties are a great addition to your breakfast sandwich. They give you a great protein punch to give you plenty of energy throughout your day. Make sure you buy a high quality vegetarian patty for the sandwich. The spinach, tomato and mushrooms combine to provide great flavor for this bagel sandwich. Have fun experimenting with different types of vegetarian sausage patties to find which ones you like the most.

Ingredients:

- 2 whole wheat bagels, sliced
- 4 slices of tomato
- 4 baby bella mushrooms, finely sliced
- 4 eggs
- 2 vegetarian sausage patties
- ½ cup of baby spinach leaves, well rinsed
- 4 tablespoons of skim milk

How to Make It:

Preheat the sandwich maker.

In a medium bowl, use a whisk to combine the milk and eggs.

Take the bottom half of one of the whole wheat bagels, placing it in the bottom of the sandwich maker.

Place 1 vegetarian sausage patty on top. Then, place ½ of the mushrooms and 2 tomato slices on top of the patty.

Pour half of the egg mixture onto the egg plate, then placing the top of the whole wheat bagel in the top slot.

Cook for five minutes and make sure the eggs are fully cooked.

Take the egg plate out of the sandwich maker, then opening it and taking the sandwich out.

Remove the top of the bagel, topping with half of the baby spinach leaves. Top with the top of the bagel.

Repeat with the remaining bagel.

Eat right away to enjoy it while it is warm.

Servings:

Makes 2 servings

Red Pepper and Spinach on Wheat

Red pepper, spinach and herb goat cheese give this sandwich a nice flavor. The tomatoes and spinach both have a lot of essential nutrients, the eggs and protein and the goat cheese is full of flavor without all the fat that comes with most other cheeses. This vegetarian breakfast sandwich is one that the entire family is going to enjoy.

Ingredients:

- 8 slices of whole wheat bread
- 12 leaves of spinach
- 4 tablespoons of herbed goat cheese
- 8 large egg whites, beaten
- 4 thin slices of green bell peppers

How to Make It:

Make sure you have the breakfast sandwich maker preheated before beginning.

Take the slices of whole wheat bread, using a large glass or a cookie cutter to cut the bread into round pieces, which makes them fit into your sandwich maker.

Take one slice of whole wheat bread, spreading it with 1 tablespoon of the herbed goat cheese. Place that piece in the bottom slot of the sandwich maker.

Add a slice of green bell pepper and 3 leaves of spinach on top of the goat cheese.

Take ¼ of the egg whites and pour into the egg slot.

Place another piece of wheat bread in the top slot.

Close the sandwich maker and cook for 5 minutes.

Remove the cooking plate, then remove the sandwich with care.

Repeat the directions for the other three sandwiches. Serve immediately for the best taste.

Servings:

Makes 4 servings

Meat Breakfast Sandwich Recipes

Adding meat to a breakfast sandwich is a great way to boost the protein you get at breakfast. Eating plenty of protein at breakfast time helps you to stay full and it also helps provide you with plenty of energy for your day. From Canadian bacon, to ham, chorizo, lox, sausage and bacon, you are sure to find a recipe that you like in this chapter. If you are trying to cut down on fat, you can also focus on choosing low fat meat choices for your sandwiches. Instead of bacon, reduce calories and fat with turkey bacon. Instead of regular sausage, consider going with a low fat turkey sausage. You can make easy exchanges to make these sandwiches even better for you if you are carefully watching your intake of calories and fat.

Follow the recipe exactly or change out a couple ingredients to make the recipe exactly to your family's taste.

Lox and Egg Breakfast Bagel

Lox and bagels is a well known combination of flavors. This sandwich recipe combines lox and bagels with eggs, making a great sandwich that offers great protein and plenty of flavor as well. Enjoy this recipe for a nice weekday breakfast, since it is easy to take the sandwich with you while you head off to work. You can also make it for a delicious brunch recipe that is wonderful for a weekend with friends and family members.

Ingredients:

- 4 wholegrain bagels, cut in half
- 6 large eggs
- ¼ cup of chive and onion spreadable cream cheese
- ¼ cup of milk
- 8 slices of smoked salmon (lox)
- Ground pepper and salt to taste

How to Make It:

Preheat the sandwich maker before working with the ingredients.

In a medium bowl, beat the milk, pepper, salt and eggs until well combined.

Take a whole grain bagel and cut it in half.

Spread the bottom half of the bagel with ¼ of the cream cheese.

Place it into the bottom slot, topping it with 2 of the salmon slices.

Take ¼ of the egg mixture and pour onto the egg pan.

Then, place the top of the bagel in the top of the sandwich maker.

Close and allow to cook for about five minutes.

Take out the egg pan and then open the maker and remove the sandwich.

Repeat the directions for the rest of the bagels.

Enjoy while warm for a delicious breakfast.

Servings:

Makes 4 servings

Canadian Bacon and Cheese Croissant

The light, flaky croissant makes this sandwich one that you will want to make again and again. The Canadian bacon adds some protein and also adds a salty sweetness to the sandwich. It is also better for you than some bacon and sausage. With the Swiss cheese and eggs, you get a great combination of flavors that will tempt your taste buds. You are sure to stay full for hours after this filling sandwich.

Ingredient:

- 2 small croissants, sliced
- 2 large eggs and 1 egg white
- 2 slices of low fat Swiss cheese
- 6 slices of Canadian bacon, pre-cooked
- 6 tablespoons of milk

How to Make It:

Preheat the sandwich maker so it can heat while you work on constructing the sandwich for cooking.

In a medium bowl, use a whisk to mix the eggs, egg white and milk together.

Slice the croissants. Then, take the bottom of one croissant, placing it into the sandwich maker.

Place a slice of Swiss cheese on top of the croissant bottom. Then, add three slices of the Canadian bacon on top of the cheese.

Pour ½ of the egg mixture on the egg pan, and then place the top of the croissant in the top of the sandwich maker.

Allow to cook for five minutes.

Remove the egg pan and then take the sandwich out, being careful so it stays together.

Repeat the process with the second croissant.

Servings:

Makes 2 servings

Parmesan and Bacon Whole Wheat Sandwich

The parmesan cheese and the bacon combine to offer incredible flavor to this sandwich. You will really enjoy the unique flavor combination. With a small bit of mayo and some tomatoes, you get a classic BLT taste with a twist, since the parmesan cheese is used. The basil ads a nice touch to the sandwich and gives you the greens instead of using lettuce. Not only is this a great breakfast sandwich recipe, but it is a sandwich you may want to make for any meal.

Ingredients:

- 8 slices of wheat bread
- 8 slices of bacon
- 2 medium tomatoes, sliced thickly
- 8 fresh basil leaves
- ¼ cup of low-fat mayonnaise
- ¾ cup of Parmesan cheese, grated and divided

How to Make It:

Take ½ cup of the parmesan cheese, dipping the bacon slices into the cheese to coat them.

On a microwave safe plate, place a paper towel, then place the bacon slices on the paper towel. Top with another paper towel. Cook in the microwave for about four minutes, or until the bacon is finished.

Preheat the sandwich maker.

In a medium bowl, combine the rest of the parmesan cheese and the mayo.

Use a cookie cutter or a large glass to cut the wheat bread into circles.

Take one piece of bread, spreading it with ¼ of the mayo mixture. Place it on the bottom of the sandwich maker.

Top with 2 slices of bacon.

Add ¼ of the tomato slices on top of the bacon.

Top with another piece of bread.

Cook for 3 minutes or until heated through.

Remove the sandwich from the sandwich maker. Then, repeat the entire process with the rest of the bread and ingredients.

Take the top off each sandwich, adding two basil leaves. Then, place the top back on the sandwich.

Serve warm.

Servings:

Makes 4 servings

Basic Bacon, Egg and Cheese Bagel

If you want just a very basic bacon, egg and cheese sandwich, this bagel recipe is for you. It's very easy to make and is a classic that nearly everyone will enjoy. Of course, you can always make it a bit different by changing the cheese, adding a bit of lettuce or adding a different breakfast meat for something a bit different.

Ingredients:

- 1 plain bagel, sliced
- 1 slices of American cheese (or you can substitute another type of cheese)
- 2 slices of cooked bacon
- 1 large egg

How to Make It:

Start by cooking the bacon until it is fully cooked and crispy.

Preheat the sandwich maker.

Take the bottom of the bagel, placing it into the bottom of the sandwich maker.

Then, place two pieces of bacon, broken in half, on the bagel bottom, topping with the American cheese.

Take the egg and crack it right into the egg slot.

Add the top of your bagel to the top slot of the sandwich maker.

Close it and then cook for about five minutes.

Take out the egg plate, then remove your sandwich.

Allow to cool for a minute or two and then enjoy while it is warm.

Servings:

Makes 1 serving

Chopped Ham and Basil Omelet Sandwich

A ham omelet is always delicious and this one adds dried basil to the eggs, giving it a delicious flavor. You can make the omelet part right in the sandwich maker, and in just minutes, you will have a great sandwich that you can enjoy in a hurry. The Cojack cheese also adds something special to this great recipe. While it makes four sandwiches, you may need to make more, since these are sure to go fast once you make them.

Ingredients:

- 4 whole wheat bagels, sliced
- 3 tablespoons of milk
- 7 eggs, well beaten
- 1 cup of ham, chopped
- 1 cup of Cojack cheese, shredded
- ½ teaspoon of dried basil
- Salt and pepper to taste

How to Make It:

Preheat the sandwich maker.

While the sandwich maker preheats, place the milk, basil, eggs, salt and pepper in a medium bowl.

Beat well to make sure ingredients are blended.

Gently stir in the chopped ham.

Cut the wheat bagels in half. Take the bottom half of one bagel, placing it in the bottom section of the breakfast sandwich maker.

Top the bagel bottom with ¼ of the shredded cheese.

Pour ¼ of the egg and ham mixture into the egg plate.

Place the top of the bagel in the top slop.

Close and cook for about five minutes, ensuring eggs are cooked.

Remove egg plate and then carefully take the sandwich out.

Repeat the process with the other three bagels.

Eat warm.

Servings:

Makes 4 servings

Chorizo and Egg English Muffin

If you enjoy Mexican food, you are sure to enjoy this delicious English muffin recipe. It combines spicy chorizo with delicious queso fresco and the smooth, creamy goodness of avocados. You will get healthy fats from the avocados, whole grains from the whole wheat English muffin and protein from the eggs in the sandwich. It is a healthy, tasty way to get the day started.

Ingredients:

- 2 whole wheat English muffins, sliced
- ½ pound of cooked chorizo
- 4 tablespoons of mild salsa
- 2 large eggs
- 1 avocado, thinly sliced
- 2 slices of queso fresco

How to Make It:

Ensure the breakfast sandwich maker is preheated.

Next, slice an English muffin and place the bottom of the muffin in the sandwich maker.

Top the English muffin bottom with half of the chorizo, then top the chorizo with a slice of queso fresco.

Take one egg and crack it right into the egg plate, then place the top of the English muffin in the top slot.

Close and cook for five minutes.

Remove the egg plate from the sandwich maker, and then, remove the sandwich.

Take the top of the sandwich off, adding ½ the avocado slices to the sandwich.

Add two tablespoons of mild salsa on top, then replace the top of the English muffin.

Repeat with the second English muffin.

Enjoy warm.

Servings:

Makes 2 servings

Healthy Turkey Bacon, Egg White English Muffin

Turkey bacon is a great substitute for regular bacon, since it has a lot less fat and calories. Turkey bacon is also delicious. Using egg whites instead of the whole egg will also help to reduce the fat and calories found in this sandwich. The recipe is really simple, but the combination of egg whites, turkey bacon and Swiss cheese is definitely delightful. It is a comforting sandwich to make on any cool morning.

Ingredients:

- 1 multigrain English muffin, sliced
- 2 large egg whites
- 1 slice of low fat Swiss cheese
- 2 slices of turkey bacon, cooked

How to Make It:

Begin by preheating the breakfast sandwich maker until the light lets you know that it is ready for you to begin making sandwiches.

Slice the multigrain English muffin in half. Take the bottom half, adding it to the bottom of the sandwich maker.

Place the slice of Swiss cheese on top of the English muffin bottom and then, add the pieces of turkey bacon, breaking if necessary to make it fit.

On the egg plate, add the two egg whites.

Then, place the muffin top in the top of the sandwich maker, closing the cover and then allowing it to cook for about five minutes.

Carefully take out the cooking plate, then open and remove the sandwich.

Eat while warm.

Servings:

Makes 1 serving

Bacon and Fried Potato English Muffin

Fried potatoes are an old-fashion breakfast staple and they really add something special to a breakfast sandwich. While you will need to make the fried potatoes before assembling the sandwich, the finished result is worth the extra time and work. With the addition of bacon, eggs and cheese, you get a full meal when you eat this breakfast sandwich. Enjoy topping it with a little ketchup or hot sauce if desired.

Ingredients:

- 4 English muffins
- 12 strips of bacon, precooked and broken in half
- 4 eggs, lightly beaten
- 4 small potatoes, cooked and thinly sliced
- ½ cup of onion, finely chopped
- 4 slices of sharp cheddar cheese
- Water for boiling
- Small amount of olive oil for frying
- Salt and pepper to taste

How to Make It:

Carefully wash the potatoes. Once washed, boil the potatoes until almost tender. Allow to completely cool. You may want to do this the night before and then place the potatoes in the refrigerator until morning.

Slice the cooked potatoes very thinly.

In a skillet, add a bit of olive oil and heat over medium heat. Add the onion and sliced potatoes to the skillet, cooking until onions are tender and potatoes are fried.

Meanwhile, fry up the bacon, placing bacon on paper towels to drain before using.

Preheat the breakfast sandwich maker.

In a small bowl, lightly beat the eggs, adding a bit of salt and pepper to taste.

Slice the English muffins. Take the bottom of one English muffin, putting in the sandwich maker on the bottom.

Place ¼ of the fried potatoes on the English muffin.

Top the potatoes with a slice of sharp cheddar cheese. Then, top with ¼ of the bacon.

Put ¼ of the egg mixture into the egg slot, then adding the top of the English muffin.

Close the machine and allow the sandwich to cook for five minutes.

Take out the egg plate and then remove the sandwich.

Allow to cool for a couple minutes and then eat while warm.

Repeat with the rest of the sandwiches.

Servings:

Makes 4 servings

Loaded Omelet Croissant

A loaded omelet is full of veggie and meat goodness. However, omelets are difficult to take with you on the go. This gives you all the delicious flavor of a loaded omelet, but it turns it into a sandwich that you can easily take with you on the way to work or while taking the kids to school. You can follow the recipe, or have fun adding in some of your favorite omelet ingredients to personalize this recipe to your own tastes.

Ingredients:

- 4 medium croissants, sliced
- 6 large eggs
- 2 slices of cooked bacon, crumbled
- ¼ cup of chopped red bell pepper
- ¼ cup of chopped red onion
- ¼ cup of chopped white button mushrooms
- ½ cup of baby spinach leaves
- ¼ cup of shredded carrots
- 1 cup of shredded low fat mozzarella cheese
- Olive oil for sautéing
- Salt and pepper

How to Make It:

In a large skillet, add a bit of olive oil and heat on medium. Add the bell pepper, red onion, mushrooms and carrots to the skillet, sautéing until the veggies are tender.

While the veggies are sautéing, add a bit of salt and pepper to the veggies.

Preheat the breakfast sandwich maker.

In a large bowl, whisk the eggs until well beaten. Add the sautéed veggies to the eggs, mixing well. Place the spinach leaves in the bowl and combine. Crumble the bacon into the egg mixture, stirring well.

Place the bottom of one croissant in the bottom slot of the breakfast sandwich maker.

Top with ¼ cup of the shredded mozzarella cheese.

In the egg slot, add a quarter of the egg mixture.

Then, add the top of the croissant to the top slot.

Close and cook for at least five minutes, ensuring the eggs are fully cooked.

Slide out the egg plate, then carefully take out the sandwich.

Repeat the same process with the rest of the omelet sandwiches.

Enjoy while hot.

Servings:

Makes 4 servings

Eggs Benedict Bagel

Eggs Benedict with a delicious hollandaise sauce can now be turned into a to-go sandwich that is easy to prepare and easy to eat. The delicious Hollandaise sauce turns a regular sandwich into something special. The addition of the baby spinach adds some essential nutrients to your breakfast and you will get plenty of protein from the eggs and the Canadian bacon used in the sandwich. This is a recipe that you will definitely want to make again and again.

Ingredients:

- 2 whole wheat bagels
- 4 slices of Canadian bacon, cooked
- 16 spinach leaves, washed and dried
- 4 large eggs, well beaten

- 3 egg yolks
- 1/8 teaspoon of cayenne
- 1 tablespoon of lemon juice
- 10 tablespoons of butter, salted

How to Make It:

In a small pot, melt the butter. Only letting it melt, ensuring that it does not begin to boil.

In a blender, add the cayenne, lemon juice and egg yolks. Blend on medium for about 30 seconds. Blending helps to add a bit of air to the yolks, making a very light hollandaise sauce. After the yolks turn lighter, place the blender on the very lowest setting, slowly drizzling in the melted butter. Allow to blend just a few seconds after all the butter is in the sauce. Set aside.

Preheat the sandwich maker.

Slice the whole wheat bagels. Take one half of the bagel, placing it in the bottom of the sandwich maker.

Take half of the spinach leaves and place on top of the bagel.

Top with two slices of Canadian bacon.

Place half of the beaten eggs in the egg cooking plate, adding the bagel top to the top slot of the appliance.

Allow to cook for five minutes.

Take out the egg plate, and then, take the sandwich out of the sandwich maker.

Take off the top of the bagel, drizzling the eggs with some of the hollandaise sauce.

Replace the top of the bagel and eat warm.

Repeat for the second bagel as well.

Servings:

Makes 2 servings

Chipotle Bacon, Egg and Cheese Biscuit

This is such a unique breakfast sandwich, full of the delicious chipotle chile pepper flavor. You can serve the sandwich up on your own homemade biscuits or you can make it easy and make biscuits from a can for this recipe. Although this sandwich requires a couple of different steps, the tasty result is well worth all of the work you put into it. Save this recipe for a leisurely weekend morning when you are not in a rush. It makes a great brunch option when you can kick back and savor the excellent flavors.

Ingredients:

- 2 biscuits, cut in half
- 2 large eggs
- 2 slices of Monterey jack cheese

- ¼ cup of cherry tomatoes, quartered
- 2 teaspoons of low fat mayo
- ¼ cup of avocado slices
- ½ lime, juiced
- 1 tablespoon of scallions, sliced
- Ground black pepper
- 1 tablespoon of fresh cilantro, minced

- 1 tablespoon brown sugar
- 2 teaspoons of red wine vinegar
- 4 slices of bacon
- 2 tablespoons of canned chipotle chile peppers in adobo sauce, minced

How to Make It:

In a skillet, cook the bacon on medium until it reaches the desired crispness.

Drain bacon on paper towels.

Remove drippings from the skillet, then add the chipotle peppers, vinegar and brown sugar to the skillet.

Simmer the glaze on medium for a minute.

Place bacon back in the pan, turning the bacon to ensure all sides of the bacon are glazed. Place in the microwave to keep the bacon warm.

For salsa, in a small bowl combine the cilantro, lime juice, avocado, pepper, tomatoes, mayo, scallions and black pepper, setting to the side.

Preheat the breakfast sandwich maker.

Place the bottom of one biscuit in the bottom slot of the sandwich maker. Top the biscuit bottom with a slice of the Monterey jack cheese.

Add two strips of the glazed bacon, broken in half, on top of the cheese.

In the egg slot, crack one of the eggs, breaking the yolk with a fork.

Add the top of the biscuit. Close and cook for five minutes.

Remove the egg plate and the sandwich.

Take the top of the biscuit off, topping with half of the salsa.

Place the top back on.

Cook the second sandwich.

Enjoy the complex, delicious flavors while warm.

Servings:

Makes 2 servings

Polish Sausage, Egg and Monterey Jack Bagel

Maybe you have never thought of using polish sausage in a breakfast recipe, but with Monterey jack cheese and eggs, the polish sausage adds wonderful flavor and plenty of protein to the sandwich. This is a sandwich that the kids will enjoy and it is really easy to make too.

Ingredients:

- 1 onion bagel, sliced
- 1 egg, beaten
- 2 thin slices of polish sausage
- 1 slice of Monterey jack pepper cheese
- 1 tablespoon of mayo
- Black pepper to taste

How to Make It:

Preheat the appliance first.

Slice the onion bagel, then spread the mayo on the bottom of the bagel.

Place the bagel with the mayo side up in the bottom of the breakfast sandwich maker.

Top with a slice of the Monterey jack pepper cheese and then place the slices of polish sausage on top of the cheese.

Pour the beaten egg into the egg plate.

Top with the other half of the bagel.

Cook for approximately five minutes.

Take out the egg plate and then take out your sandwich.

Enjoy right away.

Servings:

Makes 1 serving

Waffle and Pancake Breakfast Sandwich Recipes

Although breakfast sandwiches for sandwich makers often turn to bagels, croissants and English muffins for bread, why not have some fun using pancakes and waffles as the bread for your sandwich? These recipes are sure to be enjoyed by the kids. Most kids love waffles and pancakes, so a sandwich served up on one of their breakfast favorites will intrigue them. Have fun trying out these recipes, or use them for inspiration to come up with a few waffle and pancake breakfast sandwich recipes of your own.

Pineapple, Bacon Waffle Sandwich

This unusual sandwich brings a taste of Hawaii into your kitchen with the delicious pineapple used in the recipe. That adds a nice amount of fruit to your breakfast, and the bacon adds a great hit of protein. For the best results, make sure you use round waffles with this recipe, since they will fit best in your breakfast sandwich maker.

Ingredients:

- 8 plain waffles
- 8 slices of bacon, precooked
- 4 slices of sharp cheddar cheese
- 1 - 20 ounce can of slice pineapple, well drained

How to Make It:

Be sure to begin by ensuring your sandwich maker is preheated.

Place one waffle in the bottom slot of the appliance.

Top with two slices of pineapple.

Then, place two slices of bacon on top of the pineapple, covering the bacon with a slice of the sharp cheddar cheese.

Add another waffle to the top slot of the breakfast sandwich maker.

Cook for 3-4 minutes, or until the cheddar cheese has melted.

Repeat with the rest of the waffles.

Serve warm and enjoy the different flavors for a filling, fruity, Hawaiian breakfast.

Servings:

Makes 4 servings

Sausage, Egg and Cheese Waffle Sandwich

Whenever you have a few extra waffles around, this is a wonderful breakfast sandwich that you can throw together in no time. The waffles add a cool new flavor, which makes the sandwiches something special. Precooked sausage patties will cut down on prep time even further. Do not forget the maple syrup, since it really adds the flavor to this tasty sandwich.

Ingredients:

- 2 frozen waffles, round
- 2 large eggs, beaten
- 2 tablespoons of milk
- 1 pre-cooked sausage patty
- 1 slice of sharp cheddar cheese
- 1 tablespoon of maple syrup (use sugar free to nix the sugar content in the sandwich)

How to Make It:

In a small bowl, crack the eggs, add the milk and beat them well, setting aside.

Let the breakfast sandwich maker preheat while you are beating the eggs.

Take the waffle and put it into the bottom slot.

Take the sausage patty and place it on top of the waffle. Top with the sharp cheddar.

Pour the egg and milk mixture into the egg slot, then adding the second waffle on top.

Close and allow to cook for five minutes, ensuring that the waffles are toasted, the cheese melts and the eggs are fully cooked.

Remove the egg plate and then take out the waffle sandwich.

Serve sandwich warm with warmed maple syrup for dipping. Alternatively, you can add the syrup to the egg mixture if you want to eat this sandwich on the go without getting messy.

Servings:

Makes 1 serving

Ham, Egg, Cheese and Buttermilk Pancake Sandwich

Do not get rid of those leftover pancakes. This recipe takes leftover pancakes and turns them into a delicious sandwich that the whole family will enjoy. You can eat it with your hands on the go or you can eat it with a knife and fork if you have the time. Have fun trying your own variations of this recipe. If you already have leftover pancakes around, this recipe is a cinch and will be ready for you to enjoy in just minutes.

Ingredients:

- 2 buttermilk pancakes (leftovers or you can make fresh ones for the recipe)
- 1 egg
- 1 slice of mild cheddar cheese
- 1 slice of ham or Canadian bacon
- 2 tablespoons of maple syrup

How to Make It:

Make sure you take the time to get the breakfast sandwich maker preheating as you assemble the ingredients in the kitchen.

Take one of the pancakes, placing in the bottom of your sandwich maker.

Top with the slice of the ham or Canadian bacon. Then drizzle the syrup over the ham.

Top with the slice of the mild cheddar cheese.

Add the egg to the egg pan.

Place the remaining pancake in the top slot.

Close up the sandwich maker, cooking for five minutes or until the egg has completely finished cooking.

Remove the egg pan and then carefully remove the sandwich.

Serve warm.

Servings:

Makes 1 serving

Cream Cheese and Raspberry Waffle Sandwich

Raspberries and cream cheese are a delicious combination, especially when you combine them with buttery, crisp waffles. The addition of walnuts to the sandwich adds some healthy fats to the breakfast as well. Of course, you can easily substitute in blueberries or strawberries for the raspberries, making a variation of this recipe with the berries that you have on hand at the time. Not only is this a great sweet breakfast during the week, but it also a great option if you are serving up a brunch to guests. You can easily double or triple this recipe if you are serving these waffle sandwiches to a crowd.

Ingredients:

- 8 small, round waffles
- 2 cups of raspberries, rinsed
- 1 cup of chopped walnuts
- 8 tablespoons of the prepared raspberry cream cheese

- 2 cups of raspberries, rinse
- 3 ½ tablespoons of brown sugar
- 2 cups of cream cheese, softened at room temperature

How to Make It:

Start by making the raspberry cream cheese mixture, which you may want to make the night before. It should make enough so you have extras, allowing you to make this recipe again without having to make fresh raspberry cream cheese.

In a medium bowl, place the brown sugar and cream cheese, creaming together with a mixer for a minute or two. It should be light, smooth and creamy.

Add the two cups of raspberries to the bowl, using a large spoon to fold the berries into the cream cheese.

Refrigerate the raspberry cream cheese until firm.

Preheat the appliance before using.

Take one waffle, spreading two teaspoons of your raspberry cream cheese over the waffle.

Place inside the sandwich maker, topping with a few of the chopped walnuts.

Then, place another waffle in the top slot, allowing the sandwich to cook for about 3 minutes, ensuring all the ingredients are warm.

After cooking, take the sandwich out.

Take off the top waffle, take ½ a cup of raspberries and place them over the cream cheese mixture and walnuts.

Place the waffle back on top and enjoy the sandwich while it is still nice and warm.

Repeat with the other three sandwiches. Enjoy the sweet, delicious treat.

Servings:

Makes 4 servings

Sausage, Pancake and Syrup Sandwich

Pancakes, syrup and sausages are always a winning combination, especially if you add a bit of egg to it. This is a wonderful sandwich that can be eaten with a fork. It is a great option for mornings when you have a little more time to enjoy your breakfast. Using the 4-inch frozen pancakes really makes this an easy breakfast to make in a jiffy. Kids are sure to love this delicious combination of breakfast flavors.

Ingredients:

- 2 frozen pancakes (four-inch)
- Warm maple syrup
- 1 lightly scrambled large egg
- 1 sausage patty, precooked

How to Make It:

Preheat your appliance before using.

It is fine to use the pancakes while they are still frozen.

Take one pancake, placing in the bottom slot of your breakfast sandwich maker.

Add the sausage patty on top of the pancake.

In the cooking plate, place the beaten egg.

Top with the other frozen pancake.

Be sure to close the sandwich maker, allowing the sandwich to cook for about five minutes.

Take out the egg plate, remove the sandwich and then place on a plate.

Drizzle with warm maple syrup and eat with a fork for a warm, comforting breakfast.

Servings:

Makes 1 serving

Chicken and Bacon Waffle Sandwich

The combination of chicken and waffles has been around for years. This great breakfast sandwich combines the chicken and waffles with bacon, maple syrup and more. Although you will spend a little time getting this sandwich ready, it is so delicious and a wonderful treat. It is a wonderful option for a lazy Sunday morning. With the spicy, savory and sweet flavors, it really tempts the taste buds.

Ingredients:

- 8 round, plain, frozen waffles
- 8 chicken tenders
- 4 large eggs
- 12 slices of bacon
- Peanut oil for frying
- 1 teaspoon of dry mustard powder
- 8 slices of mild cheddar
- 1 cup of low fat mayo
- ¼ cup of heavy whipping cream
- Black pepper and salt to taste
- 1 cup of cornstarch
- 2 cups of flour
- ¼ cup of maple syrup
- 2 teaspoons of prepared horseradish
- 2 tablespoons of cayenne pepper

How to Make It:

In a large bowl, place the salt, pepper, cayenne pepper, eggs and cream. Use a whisk to whisk together until well combined.

In a plastic bag, place a dash of salt, the cornstarch and the flour. Close the bag and shake the mixture until well combined.

Take the chicken tenders, dip into the egg mixture and then place in the bag with flour mixture, shaking to make sure that the chicken fingers are well coated. Take the breaded chicken fingers and put them on a plate and allow the coating to sit for about 20 minutes.

Heat a couple inches of peanut oil in a large saucepan or a deep fryer, ensuring that the oil gets to 375 degrees F. Begin frying the chicken tenders in small batches, frying for about 6-8 minutes or until the chicken turns a golden brown. Take chicken out of the oil, allowing it to drain on a plate covered in paper towels. Keep warm in the microwave or by keeping warm within your oven.

In a small bowl, combine the mustard powder, maple syrup, mayo and horseradish.

In a skillet, cook the bacon on medium heat until crispy. Place bacon on paper towels to drain.

Preheat the sandwich maker.

Take one waffle and place it inside the sandwich maker, placing two chicken tenders on top of the waffle.

Top the chicken with three bacon slices and two cheddar slices.

Add the top waffle to the appliance.

Cook for about five minutes, making sure that the cheese is melted.

Remove from the sandwich maker.

Take off the top waffle, spreading the maple mixture on the inside of that waffle, then placing the waffle back on top.

Do the same thing for the rest of the waffles. Enjoy the chicken and waffle sandwiches while they are warm.

Servings:

Makes 4 servings

Tortilla Based Breakfast Sandwiches

Beyond traditional bread options, you can make some great breakfast sandwiches with tortillas. Both corn and flour tortillas can be used to make delicious sandwiches that are easy to grab and go in the morning. In some cases, using a tortilla to make your sandwich may help cut calories, which is an added benefit. When you are in the mood for something different for breakfast, try one of these scrumptious tortilla based breakfast sandwiches.

Mushroom, Egg and Bacon Flour Tortilla

This yummy flour tortilla sandwich is full of delicious flavors, including spinach, shiitake mushrooms and delicious apple wood-smoked turkey bacon. It makes a nutritious, filling breakfast, but you can use it for a quickly lunch recipe as well. Although the recipe makes six servings, it can be doubled if you want to serve it to a crowd for a memorable brunch dish.

Ingredients:

- 6 small flour tortillas
- 12 large eggs, well beaten
- 6 slices of turkey, apple wood-smoked bacon (about six ounces)
- 4 cups of baby spinach, washed and drained
- 4 ounces of shiitake mushrooms, sliced

How to Make It:

Start by cooking the turkey bacon in a skillet until it is nice and crispy. While cooking the bacon, set the breakfast sandwich maker to preheat.

Take the bacon out and drain on paper towels, leaving a tablespoon of the bacon drippings in the skillet. When the bacon has cooled crumble it.

Sauté the mushrooms in the drippings for about two minutes on medium.

Place the baby spinach leaves in the skillet, cooking for a minute until the leaves begin to wilt.

In a large bowl, place the 12 eggs, whisking until well beaten. Add the mushroom mixture and the crumbled bacon to the bowl, stirring to incorporate all ingredients.

Take one flour tortilla, placing it inside of the breakfast sandwich maker on the bottom.

In the egg slot, add about 1/6 of the egg mixture.

Close and cook for five minutes.

Take out the egg pan and very carefully remove the tortilla and eggs.

Roll up like a burrito and cut in half.

Repeat the process for the rest of the flour tortillas.

Eat while warm for a nutritious meal.

Servings:

Makes 6 servings

Mexican Corn Tortilla Sandwich

This Mexican corn tortilla sandwich allows you to really mix up your breakfast routine with something new. Corn tortillas are also a light lighter than many wheat breads. The beans and eggs give you plenty of protein and you will also get some great veggie nutritional goodness from the tomatoes, onions and the avocado. You can always add a bit of salsa if you want for a bit of zing.

Ingredients:

- 4 small corn tortillas
- 2 egg whites and 2 whole eggs
- ½ cup of black beans
- ½ cup of Mexican blend cheese
- ½ cup of white onions, diced
- ½ cup of tomatoes, diced
- 2 tablespoons of skim milk
- 1 cup of avocado, thinly sliced
- ¼ cup of fresh cilantro, finely chopped

How to Make It:

In a medium bowl, place the milk, the eggs and the egg whites, whisking them until well beaten.

Place the tomatoes and onions in the bowl with the eggs, mixing well until veggies are well dispersed throughout the mixture.

Preheat the sandwich maker.

In the bottom slot of the sandwich maker, place one of the corn tortillas.

Place half of the black beans on top of the tortilla, along with half of the Mexican cheese.

Pour half of the eggs into the egg slot, then add another corn tortilla on top.

Cook the tortilla for five minutes.

After taking out the egg plate, be careful when removing the sandwich.

Remove the top tortilla, topping with the slices of avocado and the cilantro.

Add salsa if desired.

Repeat the process for the second tortilla sandwich.

Eat right away and enjoy the Mexican flavors.

Servings:

Makes 2 servings

Spinach, Tomato and Egg Flour Tortilla

Flour tortillas make a great flatbread option for your breakfast sandwich. When you fill them with spinach, tomatoes and eggs, you get a well-rounded, delicious breakfast that is packed with protein and nutrients. You can always add more veggies to the tortilla if you desire, adding extra veggie goodness and nutrition.

Ingredients:

- 2 small flour tortillas
- 2 large eggs
- ¼ cup of baby spinach
- Pepper and salt to taste
- ¼ cup of cherry tomatoes, cut in half

How to Make It:

After the breakfast sandwich maker is preheated, start by placing one of the flour tortillas in the bottom slot.

Top the tortilla with the tomatoes and the baby spinach leaves.

Place two of the eggs in the egg slot, adding a dash of salt and pepper to taste, if desired.

Top with the other flour tortilla.

Cook for five minutes.

Once you have removed the egg pan, be careful when taking out the tortilla sandwich.

Repeat with the rest of the ingredients. Enjoy the tortillas immediately for the best flavor.

Servings:

Makes 1 serving

Fried Potatoes and Egg Tortilla

Fried potatoes are wonderful, but have you ever thought about putting them on your breakfast sandwich? This tortilla recipe makes use of crispy fried potatoes, but it also has eggs for protein. You may want to add some ketchup to the potatoes for extra flavor. This is a quick dish that you and the kids will enjoy eating before taking on a big day. You can even use egg substitutes in place of the eggs if you would like.

Ingredients:

- 4 yellow corn small tortillas
- 4 large eggs
- 1 cup of fried potatoes
- Pepper and salt to taste

How to Make It:

Prepare the fried potatoes the night before. You can always use leftover fried potatoes from another meal.

Preheat the appliance before you begin assembling the sandwich.

In a small bowl, place the four large eggs, whisking well until combined.

Place one small, yellow corn tortilla in the bottom of the sandwich maker, topping it with half of the fried potatoes.

In the egg slot, add half of the eggs, seasoning with a bit of salt and pepper if desired.

Add another tortilla on top.

Cook for about five minutes or until the eggs are fully cooked.

Take the egg plate from the oven and then take out the tortilla, being careful not to mess up the sandwich.

If desired, you can take off the top tortilla and add a bit of ketchup.

Repeat for the second tortilla sandwich. Eat while hot.

Servings:

Makes 2 servings

Black Bean and Corn Salsa Flour Tortilla

Black beans are not just tasty, but they also offer a lot of protein to a breakfast sandwich. This recipe has a black bean and corn salsa in it, which adds a little protein while adding plenty of flavor as well. The hard boiled eggs add even more protein to the sandwich. You get plenty of vitamins and other nutrients from the spinach leaves and the cheese melts and helps to hold everything together in this delightful sandwich that has a bit of a Mexican twist to it.

Ingredients:

- 8 small flour tortillas
- 8 hard boiled eggs, chopped
- 1 1/3 cup of black bean and corn salsa, medium hot
- 1 cup of Mexican cheese blend, shredded
- 2 cups of baby spinach leaves, rinsed and dried

How to Make It:

Chop up the hard boiled eggs, allowing the breakfast sandwich maker to begin preheating while you are doing the chopping.

Once the breakfast sandwich maker is ready, layer the first tortilla into the bottom slot.

Place ¼ of the chopped hard boiled eggs on top of the tortilla.

Place a ½ cup of the spinach on top of the eggs, then add 1/3 cup of the salsa and top with the ¼ cup of the Mexican cheese.

Then, place the top tortilla in the breakfast sandwich maker.

Heat for 3-4 minutes or until the cheese has totally melted.

Remove from the sandwich maker carefully.

Repeat the process to make the rest of the tortilla sandwiches. Serve while warm.

Servings:

Makes 4 servings

Avocado, Black Bean and Egg Corn Tortilla

This is another breakfast sandwich that has some Mexican inspiration. It makes use of delicious corn tortillas and adds a real kick with some chopped green chilies. The black beans and the eggs make sure you get a great protein punch to help you start your day with plenty of energy. The avocado adds a creamy texture to the tortilla sandwich and adds healthy fats too. This is a breakfast tortilla recipe that you are sure to make again when you want a breakfast dish with a Mexican touch.

Ingredients:

- 8 small corn tortillas (six inch)
- 4 large eggs
- 1 avocado, peeled, pitted and chopped
- 2 tablespoons of chopped green chilies
- 1 cup of canned black beans, well rinsed
- 1 cup of mild cheddar cheese, shredded

How to Make It:

Start preheating the breakfast sandwich maker, and while it is preheating you can prepare the avocado for the recipe.

After preheating, place one of the small corn tortillas into the bottom of the appliance.

Place ¼ cup of the cheese on top of the tortilla.

Then, sprinkle ¼ of the chilies on top of the cheese, topping with a quarter cup of the black beans.

Carefully break one of the eggs into a small bowl, gently dumping it into the egg plate.

Top with another corn tortilla.

Allow the sandwich to cook for about 5 minutes, but you may want to cook it for only four minutes if you want the egg over easy.

Remove the egg pan, and then you can take out the sandwich.

Remove the top tortilla, adding a quarter of the diced avocado to the tortilla sandwich, then covering it with the top corn tortilla again.

Repeat the entire process with the rest of the sandwich ingredients until all tortillas are made.

Serve while they are warm.

You may want to have sour cream on the side for dipping.

You can also add some shredded beef or chicken to the tortilla breakfast sandwiches for a bit more protein.

Servings:

Makes 4 servings

Enjoy Your New Breakfast Regime

As you can see, there are so many great recipes that you can easily make with your breakfast sandwich maker. Since you can easily make so many delightful breakfast sandwiches, it is easy to see why having a breakfast sandwich maker of your own is such a great investment. Just think of all that money you will be saving since you will no longer need to stop at the drive through in the morning.

Whether you want something with a vegetarian twist, an old favorite or a sweet treat for breakfast that makes use of fruits, you are sure to find something that you enjoy in this book of helpful recipes. Most of the recipes include healthy ingredients that will make sure that you get the proper nutrition that you need for breakfast each.

Before you know it, you will be having a great time making healthy, fast breakfast dishes for you and your family. It makes it easy to cook healthier breakfast dishes, making sure that everyone has a healthy breakfast to get the day started.

Once you have tried some of these delicious recipes for your breakfast sandwich maker, you may want to have some fun coming up with your own recipes. Try experimenting from time to time to see what works for you. Change up a few of the ingredients in the recipes here and have fun with different flavors. Over time, you may come up with family favorites that you will want to make again and again.

Printed in Great Britain
by Amazon